DEPARTMENT OF THE NAVY
HEADQUARTERS UNITED STATES MARINE CORPS
3000 MARINE CORPS PENTAGON
WASHINGTON, DC 20350-3000

I0500618

CONDUCT OF MARINE CORPS UNIT MAIL ROOMS AND MAIL DISTRIBUTION CENTERS

DEPARTMENT OF THE NAVY
HEADQUARTERS UNITED STATES MARINE CORPS
3000 MARINE CORPS PENTAGON
WASHINGTON, DC 20350-3000

MCO 5110.6C
MRP-3
JAN 21 2009

MARINE CORPS ORDER 5110.6C

From: Commandant of the Marine Corps
To: Distribution List

Subj: CONDUCT OF MARINE CORPS UNIT MAIL ROOMS AND MAIL DISTRIBUTION CENTERS

Ref: (a) DOD 4525.6-M, "DOD Postal Manual," August 15, 2002
        (b) SECNAV M-5210.1
        (c) NAVMC DIR 5210.1E
        (d) OPNAVINST 5510.1G
        (e) SECNAVINST 1640.9C

Encl: (1) Marine Corps Unit Mailrooms and Mail Distribution Centers Policies
            and procedures

1. Situation. Provide further instructions to reference (a) concerning the operation of Marine Corps Unit Mail Rooms and Mail Distribution Centers (MDC).

2. Cancellation. MCO P5110.6B.

3. Mission. This Order contains procedures for the operation of Unit Mailrooms and MDC(s).

4. Execution

    a. Commander's Intent and Concept of Operations

        (1) Commander's Intent

            (a) To prescribe policy and procedures, according to the references, for the processing and delivery of both personal and official mail for Marine Corps Unit Mailrooms and MDC(s).

            (b) The timely and accurate delivery of mail is paramount in maintaining good order throughout any unit. This Order provides the Commanding Officer with the information needed in order to operate and properly maintain an efficient Unit Mailroom and/or MDC.

        (2) Concept of Operations. The policies outlined in this Order are applicable to all Marine Corps activities that maintain a Unit Mailroom or MDC.

   b.   Subordinate Element Missions

        (1) All Marine Corps activities to include all organizations not affiliated with the Marine Corps and other entities serviced by a Marine Corps Post Office must comply with this order.

        (2) The currency, accuracy, and modification of this Order are the responsibility of the CMC (MRP-3). Commanding Officer of Marine Corps activities are responsible for the timely entry of changes and physical maintenance of their copies of this Order. Any deviation from instructions contained in this Order must be authorized by the CMC (MR).

   c.   Coordinating Instructions. Submit all recommendations concerning this Order to CMC (MRP-3) via the appropriate chain of command.

5.   Administration and Logistics

   a.   Distribution Statement "A" directives issued by CMC are published electronically and can be accessed online via the Marine Corps homepage at http://www.usmc.mil.

   b.   Access to an online medium will suffice for directives that can be obtained from the internet, CD-ROM, or other sources.

6.   Command and Signal

   a.   Command. This Order is applicable to the Marine Corps Total Force.

   b.   Signal. This Order is effective the date signed.

                                    R. S. COLEMAN
                                    Deputy Commandant for
                                    Manpower and Reserve Affairs

DISTRIBUTION: PCN 10207290500

   Copy to: JM plus 7000116 (15)
              7000095 (2)
              8145001

LOCATOR SHEET

Subj: CONDUCT OF MARINE CORPS UNIT MAIL ROOMS AND MAIL DISTRIBUTION CENTERS

Location: _____
         (Indicate the location(s) of the copy(ies) of this Order.

RECORD OF CHANGES

Log completed change action as directed.

Change Number	Date of Change	Date Entered	Signature of Person Entering Change

TABLE OF CONTENTS

TABLE OF CONTENTS

Chapter 1

General Information

1. <u>Procedures</u>

a. Commanding officers shall ensure all eligible personnel receive proper mail delivery service. These instructions apply only to letters and parcels delivered through the U.S. Postal Service (USPS), Military Postal System (MPS), and Unit Mailroom/MDC(s) herein referred to as mail.

b. All commands operating a Unit Mailroom or MDC shall use this Order for standardized mail processing, distribution, and delivery procedures. This Order amplifies the information contained in reference (a) and is the authority for Marine Corps Unit Mailroom and MDC operations.

2. <u>Mail Service</u>. The commanding officer will ensure personal mail is properly delivered to the members of the command. The receipt of personal mail through the Unit Mailroom or MDC is restricted to personnel residing in military barracks where USPS does not deliver mail. Marines residing in military housing or in off-base quarters where USPS delivers are not authorized to receive personal mail through the Unit Mailroom/MDC, and may not use their military address to receive bank statements, credit card invoices, or magazine subscriptions. However, installation commanders may grant exemption when considered necessary for the timely deliver of mail. Recently transferred personnel not residing in the barracks may use their military address until they establish permanent quarters. In doing so, they must notify their correspondents of a permanent address within 90 days after joining the command. Any mail received after the 90 day period will be returned to sender or forwarded to the service member's residence with an appropriate endorsement.

3. <u>Definitions</u>

a. <u>Accountable Mail</u>. A general term used to describe mail that provides special services: Express Mail Military Service (EMMS), registered, certified, insured with signature, and return receipt.

b. <u>Unit Postal Officer</u>. An Officer, Warrant Officer, Staff Non-Commissioned Officer or civilian employee (GS-6 or above), designated in writing by the unit commander to supervise the operation of the Unit Mailroom or MDC.

c. <u>Assistant Unit Postal Officer</u>. An Officer, Warrant Officer, Staff Non-Commissioned Officer or civilian employee (GS-6 or above) designated in writing by the commander to assist the unit postal officer in the supervision of the Unit Mailroom/MDC.

d. <u>Unit Mail Clerk</u>. An individual designated on DD Form 285 (Appointment of Military Postal Clerk, Unit Mail Clerk, or Mail Orderly) and maintain DD Form 2260 (Unit Mail Clerk/Orderly Designation Log) by proper authority to perform mail handling duties in the operation of a Unit Mailroom or MDC.

e. <u>Unit Mail Orderly</u>. An individual designated on DD Form 285 by proper authority to pick up mail from the MPO, Unit Mailroom or MDC and deliver it to the addressee.

f. <u>Unit Mail Room</u>. A properly secured room or enclosure established at a battalion, squadron, or separate company level which serves as a place for mail clerks to keep the mail safe and secure, process, and deliver mail to mail orderlies or other authorized personnel.

g. <u>Back Stamp</u>. A date stamp applied to the back of a piece of mail to indicate the date of receipt.

h. <u>Depredation</u>. An act of unlawfully tampering with mail with the intent to steal, damage, or in any way prevent the timely and secure delivery of mail.

i. <u>Mail Distribution Center</u>. A secure area where mail delivery is accomplished through assigned mail receptacles or section mail call.

j. <u>Marine Corps Mail Room</u>. Mail rooms operated by Marine Corps postal clerks who, in conjunction with civilian U.S. postal clerks, provide postal support and are located in the same building. Civilian U.S. postal clerks provide all financial operations, accountable mail control, mail dispatch, and receipt points for the MCMR.

k. <u>Marine Corps Postal Clerk</u>. A Marine who receives formal training and is officially designated (MOS 0161) on DD Form 2257 (Designation/Termination MPC-FPC-Cope-PFO) to perform postal functions in the operation of a Military Post Office (MPO). Postal clerks will not be assigned to perform Unit Mailroom or MDC duties.

l. <u>Military Post Office (MPO)</u>. Post offices operating as an extension of the USPS by armed forces personnel to serve and perform all postal functions for designated military bases.

m. <u>Official Mail</u>. Any letter, publication, or parcel relating exclusively to the business of the U.S. Government, which is mailed using official postage. Additionally, mail that has an official return address, uses a government agency's indicia, contains a military title in the address, or is addressed to the "Commandant of the Marine Corps," "Commanding General," "Commanding Officer," "Executive Officer," "Adjutant," "Commanding Officer of _____," or the Officer in charge is considered official mail.

n. <u>Ordinary Mail</u>. All mail that is not classified as accountable mail.

o. <u>Postal Inspector</u>. A Marine Corps postal officer MOS 0160 or enlisted MOS 0161, members of the Inspector General of the Marine Corps (IGMC) team, or major command inspection teams (MARFORCOM/PAC), Commanding General Inspection Program (CGIP) or installation postal team, for the purpose of conducting audits and inspections of MPO(s), PSC(s), Official Mail Management Programs, Unit Mailrooms/MDC(s) within their Area Of Responsibility.

p. Marine Corps Postal Officer. A Marine Corps officer assigned MOS 0160 who manages installation MPO operations, conducts audits, and investigations on any command related postal matters.

q. Unit. Any Marine Corps organization or activity that operates a Unit Mailroom or MDC for providing delivery of mail.

4. Responsibilities

a. Commanding officers shall:

(1) Provide adequate space and equipment necessary for proper mail handling and security, and ensure mail clerks and mail orderlies have sufficient time to perform their duties.

(2) Report and take action on postal offenses and losses per reference (a) of this Order.

(3) Appoint individuals in writing to receipt for all official mail.

(4) Appoint Unit Postal Officer(s) and an Assistant Unit Postal Officer(s) by either letter or unit special order.

b. Unit Postal Officer(s) or Assistant Postal Officer(s) shall:

(1) Ensure unit mail clerks attend local military post office mail clerk indoctrination classes within 30 days of being appointed mail handling duties.

(2) Ensure unit mail orderlies receive unit level training on mail handling procedures prior to assuming mail handling duties.

(3) Ensure mail is properly handled and delivered in compliance with reference (a) and this Order.

(4) Ensure the Unit Mailroom/MDC is operated in compliance with reference (a) and this Order.

(5) Conduct random weekly unannounced mail room inspections.

(6) Notify the commander and serving post office of all suspected or known postal offenses or losses.

(7) Verify daily that all official accountable mail (Express, Registered, Certified, Numbered Insured, Return receipt for Merchandise Mail) has been properly delivered by initialing PS Form 3883 (Firm Delivery Book Registered, Certified, and Numbered Insured Mail).

(8) Control and secure duplicate keys or combinations to the Unit Mailroom/MDC.

(9) Issue and revoke all DD Form 285. These forms are available on the DOD Forms website:

(http://www.dtic.mil/whs/directives/infomgt/forms/formsprogram.htm).

(10) Ensure the mail directory file cards and mail processing records are properly maintained.

(11) Attend training prior to assuming Unit Postal Officer & Assistant Unit Postal Officer duties.

c. Unit mail clerks shall:

(1) Operate the Unit Mailroom/MDC per reference (a) and this Order.

(2) Safeguard mail in their possession.

(3) Ensure entry to the Unit Mailroom/MDC is limited to authorize individuals.

(4) Perform directory service on all undeliverable mail and return it to the servicing post office at the next mail call.

(5) Attend local military post office mail clerk indoctrination classes within 30 days of being appointed mail handling duties.

(6) Back stamp all mail that is received in the Unit Mailroom/MDC to show date of receipt.

(7) Ensure official mail is delivered to the addressee or to the authorized agent designated in writing by the commanding officer to receipt for official mail.

(8) Report known or suspected postal violations to the Unit Postal Officer or the Assistant Unit Postal Officer.

d. Unit mail orderlies shall:

(1) Pick up mail at specified times and safeguard it at all times.

(2) Ensure personal mail is delivered only to the addressee or an authorized agent. Delivery to addressee's OIC/NCOIC for subsequent delivery is not authorized.

(3) Official mail will be delivered to the addressee or to an agent authorized by the commanding officer to receipt for such mail.

(4) Return all undeliverable mail to the Unit Mailroom the same day it is received with supporting documentation stating the reason it could not be delivered. (i.e., leave, TAD, etc.)

(5) Report known or suspected postal violations to the Unit Postal Officer or the Assistant Unit Postal Officer.

(6) Attend unit level training on mail handling procedures prior to assuming mail handling duties.

Chapter 2

Administration

1. Required References. Each Unit Mailroom/MDC is required to maintain a copy of the most current edition of the required publications/directives. If the Unit Mailroom is equipped with a computer, electronic versions of these publications/directives are authorized, i.e., CD, Internet, etc. The below listed references are required to be maintained in the Unit Mailroom/MDC:

    a. DOD 4525.6-M, Department of Defense Postal Manual.

    b. OPNAVINST 5112.6D Navy Postal Instruction.

    c. MCO 5110.6C Conduct of Marine Corps Unit Mail Rooms and Mail Distribution Centers.

    d. Base Order for Postal Affairs.

    e. Unit Mail Handling Order.

2. Mail Handling Order. All commands operating a Unit Mailroom/MDC must publish mail handling instructions that provide personnel with sufficient information about local mail service. These instruction, at a minimum, will include the following:

    a. The correct and complete mailing address used by personnel attached to the command.

    b. The location and hours of operation of the Unit Mailroom/MDC, and servicing post office.

    c. The location and collection hours for outgoing mail receptacles.

    d. Mail call hours and mail distribution procedures.

    e. Instructions for using OPNAV 5110/5 (Change of Address Card).

    f. Information about security of mail and postal effects.

    g. Procedures to establish a classified material screening point.

    h. Non-Mailable Items

        (1) Any article or material that can harm people or property.

        (2) Liquor.

        (3) Obscene matter.

        (4) Libelous matter.

(5) Subversive matter.

(6) Lottery materials or any written or printed matter intended to swindle or defraud.

(7) Concealable firearms, explosives, shell casings, and unsheathed knives and swords.

i. Procedures for handling mail for personnel temporarily absent from the command.

3. <u>Mail Room No Admittance Except To Authorized Personnel</u>. All Unit Mailroom/MDC(s) will prominently display DD Form 1115 (Mail Room No Admittance Except to Authorized Personnel) on or near the entrance to the Unit Mailroom/MDC indicating the hours of operation and an example of a correct mailing address for the command. (See Figure 2-1).

4. <u>Space And Equipment</u>. All Unit Mailroom/MDC(s) will be constructed per Chapter 3 of this Order and contain enough space to accommodate a desk, computer, filing cabinet, mail sorting case, bag rack and an area to process mail unencumbered. Only U.S. mail, postal records, and essential furniture will be in the Unit Mailroom/MDC. Personal items such as cassette/CD players, television sets, and video games will not be permitted in the Unit Mailroom/MDC. The Unit Mailroom/MDC will not be used to store other gear that is not related to the delivery or processing of mail. The Unit Mailroom/MDC will be kept clean, neat, and organized in an orderly manner.

5. <u>Prohibitions</u>. Mail clerks will not open, read, or store personal mail addressed to them in the Unit Mailroom/MDC. Mail clerks will not receive, store in the unit mail room, or deliver packages received from couriers not affiliated with USPS (i.e., Federal Express, United Parcel Service, etc.).

6. <u>Unit Mailroom/MDC Inspections</u>

a. Unit postal officer(s)/assistant postal officer(s) will conduct weekly inspections using the current edition of the Automated Inspection Reporting System (AIRS) Checklist. Inspections will be conducted unannounced and at random so as not to establish a trend when inspections are accomplished. Weekly unannounced inspection AIRS Checklists for Unit Mailroom/MDC(s) may be destroyed after the unit has been inspected by the MPO or command designated representatives each quarter. Quarterly mail inspections AIRS Checklists for Unit Mailroom/MDC(s) should be kept on file in the Unit Mailroom/MDC for two years.

b. The command postal officer, MPO supervisor of the serving postal facility, or a command designated representative (if no MPO supervisor is in the area) will conduct unannounced inspections of all Unit Mailroom/MDC(s) served by the command at least quarterly, using the AIRS Checklist. All Unit Mailroom/MDC(s) receiving a non-mission capable rating during a quarterly inspection will be inspected monthly until they receive at least two consecutive ratings of "mission capable." Marine Corps mail rooms operated by Marine Corps personnel in conjunction with a civilian post office shall be inspected annually.

c. Personnel augmenting an IGMC inspection team or other designated USMC inspection teams may inspect Unit Mailrooms, MDC(s), MCMR(s), and MPO(s) as directed. In addition to Marine Corps inspectors, USPS postal inspectors may also inspect Unit Mailrooms, MDC(s), MCMR(s), and MPO(s) on request from or on approval of the responsible commander.

d. Proper identification is required prior to granting access to mail handling areas.

e. Inspector-Instructor staffs, officer selection offices, and recruiting stations that do not maintain Unit Mailroom/MDC(s) will not be inspected by an IGMC team as a Unit Mailroom/MDC. IGMC inspectors should only include the inspection of Official Mail Management procedures for these types of units and review the procedures of personal mail delivery if the unit receives personal mail.

7. <u>Postal Inspector</u>. A Marine Corps postal inspector will be identified by a NAVMC 11157 (Marine Corps Postal Inspector Identification Card). This NAVMC card will be issued to all Marine Corps postal personnel who inspect mail handling facilities and military post offices. The back of the card will identify the major commands to be inspected and assigned inspection responsibilities. Postal inspectors should retain the NAVMC 11157 card on their person at all times until they are relieved as postal inspectors. NAVMC 11157 can be obtained from the CMC (MRP-3).

8. <u>Designation Procedures</u>. The unit postal officer or assistant unit postal officer shall use a DD Form 285 (Appointment of Military Postal Clerk, Unit Mail Clerk, or Orderly) to designate all mail clerks and orderlies within their command. This form is available on the DOD Forms website: **(http://www.dtic.mil/whs/directives/infomgt/forms/formsprogram.htm**. The unit postal officer and assistant unit postal officer will be designated in writing by the commanding officer. If a unit postal officer/assistant postal officer is actually involved in handling mail then they will also complete a DD Form 285. Unit postal officers, assistant unit postal officers, mail clerks, and mail orderlies will receive mail handling training prior to assignment to mail handling duties.

9. <u>Mail Clerk and Orderly Designations</u>. The command will keep the number of designated mail clerks and orderlies to a minimum to allow efficient and effective handling and delivery of the mail. A minimum of two mail clerks and orderlies should be appointed per each unit or section.

a. <u>DD Form 285</u>. Three original DD Forms 285 shall be prepared for each mail clerk. One will be retained in the Unit Mailroo, one will be provided to the servicing MPO or local USPS, and the mail clerk will retain one copy with him/her at all times when performing mail handling duties. MPO and Unit Mailroom will retain DD Form 285 in accordance with reference (b) SSIC 5510.1A. Two DD Forms 285 will be prepared for each company/section mail orderly. One copy will be retained in the Unit Mailroom /MDC, and the mail orderly will retain one copy with him/her at all times when performing mail handling duties. DD Forms 285 will be typewritten or neatly handwritten. It is highly encouraged to have DD Forms 285 laminated for durability. Mail clerks/orderlies will also have with them their DD Form 2/CAC (Armed Forces ID Card) for active duty personnel or appropriate additional identification for civilian personnel when performing mail handling duties. Figure 2-2 shows a properly completed DD Form 285. Prepare the DD Form 285 as follows:

(1) Block 1 - Effective date (actual date the card is signed by the appointing official).

(2) Block 2 - Disregard date revoked and assign a sequential accountable number for each card. (e.g., 2-08 or 002-08 per Figure 2-2).

(3) Block 3 - Last name, first name, middle initial.

(4) Block 4 - Rank/Pay Grade.

(5) Block 5 - Not required.

(6) Block 6 - Title (Mail Clerk or Mail Orderly).

(7) Block 7 - Enter the mail clerks organization or the mail orderlies section.

(8) Block 8 - City, State, and zip code where unit is located.

(9) Block 9 - Indicate the type of mail a clerk is authorized to pick up by placing an "x" in the appropriate box. Mail clerks and orderlies are only authorized to pick up "PERSONAL (except accountable)", "OFFICIAL (ALL)", or "OFFICIAL (except accountable)" mail. They are not authorized to pick up "PERSONAL (ALL)" mail. The appointing official will also initial each section to validate the authorization.

(10) Block 10 - The MPO will use the All Purpose Date Stamp to validate all DD Forms 285 for mail clerks. This block will be left blank for orderlies who pick up mail from the Unit Mailroom/MDC and the appointing official's initials in block 9 will validate the card.

(11) SIGNATURE OF APPOINTING OFFICIAL - The unit postal officer or assistant unit postal officer will sign each DD Form 285 in this block.

(12) SIGNATURE OF APPOINTEE - The mail clerk or orderly will sign each DD Form 285 in this block.

(13) When a mail clerk is relieved of duty/revoked, a letter of revocation, along with a copy of their DD Form 285, will be provided to the servicing post office. An appropriate entry will be made in DD Form 2260 (Unit Mail Clerk/Orderly Designation Log) indicating revocation.

(14) When a mail orderly is relieved of duty/revoked, an appropriate entry will be made in DD Form 2260 indicating revocation and all copies of DD Forms 285 will be destroyed.

b. DD Form 2260 (Unit Mail Clerk/Orderly Designation Log)

(1) DD Form 2260 is used to record all mail clerk/orderly appointments. All information on this log, including the appointing official's signature, must coincide with the information contained on the DD

Form 285. When the individual is authorized to receipt for accountable mail, an asterisk, or some other notation, is placed in the left margin. Unit mail clerk/orderly numbers will be assigned sequentially and will coincide with the number on their DD Forms 285. DD Form 2260 (Rev. 5-00) is available from the DOD Forms website:

(http://www.dtic.mil/whs/directives/infomgt/forms/formsprogram.htm).

(2) DD Form 2260 will be retained per reference (b) SSIC 5110.13a and 13b as appropriate. Figure 2-3 shows a properly completed DD Form 2260.

(3) The mail clerk is responsible for the maintenance of DD Form 2260 and the unit postal officer will ensure the accuracy of DD Form 2260 on a weekly basis.

10. <u>Training</u>. Commanding officers will ensure unit postal officers, mail clerks and mail orderlies are knowledgeable in all aspects of mail handling operations and properly trained in their responsibilities prior to designation. Unit mail clerks are required to attend the local military post office mail clerk indoctrination course within 30 days of assuming mail handling duties. Unit postal officers and Assistant Postal Officers are highly encouraged to attend. Once a unit mail clerk transfers to a new duty station, he or she must attend the mail clerk indoctrination course for his or her new command. Section mail orderlies must attend unit level training prior to assuming mail handling duties. Commands may use locally developed military postal programs to satisfy this requirement.

MAIL ROOM

NO ADMITTANCE
EXCEPT TO AUTHORIZED PERSONNEL

MAIL CALL

DAILY	SATURDAY	SUNDAY & HOLIDAYS
0800 – 1600	N/A	N/A

THIS NOTICE IS TO BE ATTACHED TO MAIL ROOMS

DD Form 1115, MAR 56

Figure 2-1.--(Mailroom No Admittance Except to Authorized Personnel /Example
of Correct Military Address)

APPOINTMENT OF MILITARY POSTAL CLERK, UNIT MAIL CLERK OR MAIL ORDERLY *(See Instructions on Reverse)*	1. DATE EFFECTIVE 071004	2. DATE REVOKED 2-08

3. NAME OF APPOINTEE *(Last, First, Middle Initial)*

Smith John W

4. NAME OR GRADE LCpl	5. SSN N/R	6. TITLE OF APPOINTEE Mail Clerk

7. ORGANIZATION/ACTIVITY CSSG-3	8. APO, MPO, OR CONUS INSTALLATION MCBH KANEHOHE BAY HI 96863

9. **MAIL AUTHORIZED TO RECEIVE** *(Check and Initial)*	10. THIS FORM MUST BE VALIDATED BY THE SERVING AGENCY'S GENERAL PURPOSE DATING STAMP PRIOR TO CLERK RECEIVING MAIL. IN THE CASE OF THE NAVY MOBILE UNITS, VALIDATION MAY BE BY IMPRESSION OF THE OFFICIAL SEAL.

PERSONAL *(ALL)* ☐	OFFICIAL *(Except accountable)* ☐
PERSONAL *(Except accountable)* ☒ P.O. Initials	OFFICIAL POUCHES ONLY ☐
OFFICIAL *(ALL)* ☒ P.O. Initials	☐

SIGNATURE OF APPOINTING OFFICIAL **I. M. Postal Officer**	SIGNATURE OF APPOINTEE **John W. Smith**

DD FORM 285, JUN 67

(FRONT)

Item 6. Indicate the correct title of the appointee: Military Postal Clerk, Unit Mail Clerk or Mail Orderly.

Item 7. State the exact activity, i.e., Sq, Gp, Ship's Name, BN, CO, BSO, NCO Club, Exchange, Official Center, etc.

Item 9&10. Appointing official will check box and initial by each type of mail appointee is authorized to receive.
Validating official will enter his initials in lower right hand corner.

Signature of Appointing Official – I have appointed the individual named to receive mail indicated addressed to the specific organization/activity shown. When this appointment is terminated, I will (1) Notify the agency through which mail is received, (2) Destroy DD 285 returned by the individual, and (3) Complete Item 2 (DD 285) on the Unit File Copy and retain it for the period specified in the applicable service's regulation.

Signature of Appointee – I have studied the instructions in applicable regulations, manuals and other directives, and am thoroughly familiar with my responsibilities and duties. I will carry this authorization whenever I am engaged in mail handing duties and return it to the appointing official when I am relieved of mail handling duties.

(BACK)

Figure 2-2.--DD Form 285 (Appointment of Military Postal Clerk, Unit Mail Clerk or Mail Orderly)

UNIT MAIL CLERK/ORDERLY DESIGNATION LOG

1. Card No.	2. Date Issued (Yr, Mo, Day)	3. Date Revoked (Yr, Mo, Day)	4. Activity Identifier	5. Name of Designee (Print) Last, First, MI	6. Designee (Signature)	7. Appointing Official (Signature)	8. Pay Grade
1-08	20070218	20071024	HQBN	I.M. Mailclerk	I.M. Mailclerk	I.M. Postal Officer	CAPT
2-08	20071004		CSSG-3	Smith, John W.	John W. Smith	I.M. Postal Officer	CAPT

DD Form 2260, MAY 2000

PREVIOUS EDITIONS ARE OBSOLETE

Figure 2-3.--DD Form 2260 (Unit Mail Clerk/Orderly Designation Log)

Chapter 3

Security

1. General

a. Unit Mail Clerks and Section Mail Orderlies shall safeguard mail in their possession at all times and may be held liable for failure to handle mail properly. The Unit Mailroom/MDC will be locked when the mail clerk is not present.

b. The following are minimum structural requirements for a Unit Mailroom/MDC located in a permanent structure:

(1) All locks and door hinges will be mounted inside or in such a manner to prevent easy removal. Spot welding the door hinges is highly recommended to prevent easy access.

(2) All windows will be barred or covered with heavy wire mesh to prevent easy access from the outside.

(3) Walls and ceilings will be constructed to prevent forcible entry.

(4) Receptacles (if used) will be installed to prevent access to or from other receptacles or a customer service window.

c. When conducting training in the field or in a deployed environment, every effort will be made by the command to provide 24-hour security of the mail.

2. Access. Only authorized personnel are allowed to enter the Unit Mailroom/MDC (e.g., Commanding Officer, Executive Officer, Postal Officer, Inspectors, and supervised working parties). The Mail Clerk must verify identification and authorization of all personnel prior to allowing entry into the Unit Mailroom/MDC and must remain there until all authorized personnel conclude their business and depart.

3. Control of Keys or Combinations

a. Postal Officers will determine which mail clerk will be issued the key or combination to the Unit Mailroom/MDC.

b. The Mail Clerk authorized a Unit Mailroom/MDC key will possess only one key and safeguard it at all times. The mail clerk will sign a key log indicating they have been issued a key to the Unit Mailroom/MDC.

c. The duplicate key or combination to the Unit Mailroom/MDC shall be sealed in a plain envelope or a PS Form 3977 "Duplicate Key Envelope" (Figure 3-1), which can be obtained through your servicing post office and kept in a safe controlled by the Postal Officer or a representative designated by the commanding officer. The Mail Clerk holding the original key and the Postal Officer will both sign across the back flap of the envelope and endorse the front of the envelope to show its contents and date sealed. Prior to sealing the duplicate key in the key envelope, ensure the key works properly. A new envelope will be prepared whenever the duplicate key or combination is used.

4. Transporting Mail

a. Commands shall transport all mail to and from the servicing postal facility area in a closed-body military vehicle equipped with lockable doors. If such a vehicle is unavailable, mail clerks or orderlies will ride in the compartment with the mail or at least maintain visual contact with the mail. If the situation arises that a military vehicle is not available, the unit may request authorization to use a privately owned vehicle. The request will be made by the unit Postal Officer and approved by the servicing post office.

b. USPS equipment will only be used to transport mail, excluding oversize pieces. USPS equipment will be returned to the servicing post office when not needed to accomplish the mission of the Unit Mailroom/MDC.

5. Security of Mail and Postal Records

a. The privacy of mail and mail records shall not be violated. Mail clerks and orderlies shall not break the seal of any mail matter nor are they to release any information about mail or mail records. Requests for information will be referred to the unit postal officer.

b. Personal addresses of all personnel are privileged information and will not be divulged to anyone except in the course of official business. Mail clerks will refuse all telephone inquiries and "third party" requests for personal addresses.

6. Hazardous Mail Training

a. Security of mail and mail handlers is paramount. Lessons learned from the September 11th bombing of the World Trade Center in 2001 have prompted the MPS to create an active role of all mail handlers to identify suspicious mail. As such, training all mail handling personnel to identify hazardous mail and how to ensure its safe handling is directed. Post office personnel will coordinate with local hazardous material personnel, law enforcement and fire department officials, and medical personnel to ensure training of all mail handlers is accomplished annually. Training at a minimum will be focused on detection of mail bombs, isolation of packages, evacuation procedures, and identifying biological and chemical hazardous mail. Personnel to be trained are postal clerks, unit mail clerks, section mail orderlies, and official mail sections.

b. Supplemental mail handling instructions will be provided by DoD, HQMC, and USPS as incidents occur.

7. Emergency Destruction of Mail and Postal Records

a. Destruction plans of all Marine Corps activities operating Unit Mailroom/MDC(s) shall include instructions for disposing of mail and equipment in emergencies involving danger or capture, as follows:

(1) When sufficient advanced warning is received:

(a) Deliver to addressee or dispatch mail on hand to the nearest postal facility by the safest and most expeditious means available, and

(b) Suspend operations and transport mail handling effects and supplies to a safe area.

(2) When there is insufficient advance warning, emergency destruction of mail shall take place in the following order:

(a) Official registered mail.

(b) Directory service records.

(c) Other accountable mail.

(d) All remaining mail.

(e) Other records, equipment, mail sacks, furniture, etc.

b. If possible, the postal officer and assistant postal officer will witness the destruction of mail handling effects. When the assigned postal officers are not available, witnesses should include two officers when possible, or one officer and one senior enlisted person, or two enlisted personnel of any grade.

c. Personnel conducting emergency destruction shall submit a list of items destroyed to the CMC (MRP-3) within 48 hours.

EMPLOYEE (Print Last Name, First Name and Middle Initial)

OPERATING UNIT

CSSG-3

EQUIPMENT	NO.	NO. KEYS	SERIAL NO.
CASH DRAWER			
Mail room		1	64125
STAMP CABINET			
SAFE COMPARTMENT			
ENVELOPE DRAWER			

DESIGNATED WITNESS (Print)

1. I. M. POSTAL OFFICER

2. I. M. MAIL CLERK

INSTRUCTIONS: After enclosing the duplicate keys, the employee to whom assigned and the witness to the sealing of the envelope by the employee shall sign across both flaps on the back of the envelope. A distinct and legible postmark should be affixed across both envelope flaps. Envelope containing duplicate keys shall be assigned to the appropriate supervisor, who will be held personally responsible for their protection.

If necessary to temporarily withdraw keys for use by the employee to whom assigned, this envelope shall be opened by the employee in the presence of a witness, endorsed by both, dated and preserved. When the keys are returned, the opened envelope should be discarded and a new envelope prepared.

If necessary to have access to a receptacle assigned to an employee absent from duty, the supervisor responsible for the duplicate key will withdraw the keys from this envelope in the presence of one of the designated witnesses, and each will endorse this envelope to show date and reason for withdrawing the keys. An inventory of the credit thus made accessible shall be made and certified by the supervisor, or other designated employee, and the witness and maintained by the supervisor together with the opened envelope. (See Section 378, Handbook F-1).

DUPLICATE KEY ENVELOPE

3977

PS Form
Oct 1979

(FRONT)

I. M. Mailclerk
(Mail Clerk's Signature and Date)

I. M. Postal Officer
(Postal Officer or Asst PO Signature and Date)

(BACK)

Figure 3-1.--PS Form 3977 (Duplicate Key Envelope)

Chapter 4

Mail Handling

1. General. Mail Clerks and Orderlies shall safeguard mail at all times and may be held liable for any loss caused by their failure to handle the mail properly.

2. Personal Mail

    a. Reference (a) prohibits using Department of Defense personnel and resources to duplicate services that USPS provides. All personnel residing in housing or billeting where USPS delivers mail will receive personal mail at their quarters. Personally addressed mail is considered official when the address includes a duty title or when sent in an official envelope with the Marine Corps or DoD activity paying the postage. Installation Commanders may grant exception to duplication of services for those service members, who because of their assignment or whose duties prohibit their ability to receive mail daily at their quarters address.

    b. Unit Mail Clerks and Orderlies are not authorized to handle personal accountable mail. Mail clerks will pick up a PS Form 3849 "Deliver/Notice/Receipt" (Figure 4-1) from the servicing post office and deliver it to the individual or the responsible mail orderly. Individuals are responsible for picking up their own accountable mail and cannot appoint mail clerks or orderlies as agents in this regard. Exceptions to this policy can be made if the unit is located in a remote area where the individual service member does not have access or transportation to the post office where the accountable mail is held. Requests for the exception to this policy will be submitted in writing by the Unit Postal Officer to the Installation Postal Officer for approval.

    c. Postage due and Collect On Delivery services are not available in Unit Mailroom/MDC(s). Mail Clerks will handle postage due as regular mail. Should mail clerks receive COD mail at the Unit Mailroom/MDC, they will return this mail to the servicing post office for processing.

    d. Mail Clerks are required to back stamp all mail upon receipt from the servicing post office to reflect a date of receipt.

    e. Mail addressed to Unit Mail Clerks will not be opened, stored, or disposed of within the Unit Mailroom/MDC.

    f. Mail Clerks and Orderlies will give balloting material priority handling.

    g. Addressees may refuse mail they do not want. The addressee will write on the front of the envelope or wrapper "REFUSED", sign, and date it. IF the addressee declines to make the endorsement, the mail clerk/orderly will endorse it "REFUSED BY ADDRESSE", sign, date, and return it to the servicing post office.

h. Mail Clerks and Orderlies will immediately report any mail suspected of containing harmful matter or controlled substances to the unit postal officer and servicing post office.

i. When mail has been opened by mistake, the mail clerk/orderly will instruct the individual to reseal the envelope, endorse it "OPENED BY MISTAKE", and sign it. The mail clerk/orderly will then return the mail envelope to the servicing Unit Mailroom/MDC or post office for proper disposition.

j. When Marines are temporarily absent from their unit, mail will be handled as follows:

(1) Mail for personnel on leave or TAD for 30 days or less will be held in the Unit Mailroom/MDC. The Unit Mailroom/MDC is required to maintain documentation on hand showing leave or TAD dates for all mail being held. When personnel return from TAD or leave the mail shall be delivered and the required documentation showing leave or TAD dates will not be required to be maintained in the Unit Mailroom/MDC. Service members may choose to have their mail forwarded during this time. The service member must provide a letter to the Unit Mailroom/MDC providing a forwarding address, along with a stop date, and a signature of authorization to forward mail. This letter will be kept on file in the Unit Mailroom/MDC and will be destroyed when the service member returns.

(2) Mail for personnel TAD for greater than 30 days will be forwarded until 1 week prior to the designated return date, unless otherwise requested. This allows the individual ample time to effect delivery of the mail being forwarded prior to retuning to the unit. Service members may choose to have their mail held in the Unit Mailroom/MDC while TAD for greater than 30 days, but no longer than 60 days. The service member must provide a letter to the Unit Mailroom/MDC showing authorization to hold mail. The letter must state when the service member leaves for TAD and when he or she is due to come back from TAD, along with a signature of authorization. Mail held past 60 days for personnel in a TAD status will be returned to sender with the endorsement "MOVED LEFT NO FORWARDING ADDRESS."

k. Mail for transferred personnel will be handled per Chapter 6 of this Order.

l. Mail that is received at the Unit Mailroom/MDC that is open, damaged, or missing contents will be endorsed with the appropriate endorsement by the mail clerk; "RECEIVED IN OPEN CONDITION", "RECEIVED IN DAMAGED CONDITION", "RECEIVED WITHOUT CONTENTS", with the date of receipt and the identity of the unit endorsing the article of mail.

3. Official Mail. Mail Clerks and Orderlies shall safeguard official mail in the same manner as personal mail.

a. Official mail shall only be delivered to an authorized agent of the command whom has been designated in writing by the Commanding Officer to receive official mail addressed to that command.

b. Official mail such as MCI mail, master brief sheets, official surveys addressed to the individual service member as personal mail will be delivered as addressed to the individual service member whenever possible. These types of official mail for personnel who have transferred will be forwarded to the forwarding address provided or returned to sender with the appropriate endorsement, if no forwarding address was provided.

c. Accountable Mail

(1) Commanding Officers shall designate in writing personnel authorized to receipt for and open official accountable mail. The authorization letter must be signed by the current Commanding Officer only. "By Direction" authority is not authorized. The authorization letter will contain a sample signature of the all individuals authorized to sign for and open official mail addressed to the Commanding Officer (Figure 4-2). A single letter may authorize more than one individual; however, any change to the authorization letter will require cancellation of the previous letter and publishing of a new letter. Authorization letters will be maintained per reference (b) SSIC 5110.1b.

(2) A chain of receipts shall cover all accountable mail from acceptance by the Mail Clerk through delivery to addressee or authorized agent. The mail clerk must be able to account for all accountable mail either by producing the article or by showing delivery of the article to the addressee or authorized agent.

(3) The servicing post office shall prepare PS Form 3883 "Firm Delivery Receipt for Accountable and Bulk Delivery Mail" (Figure 4-3) in triplicate and keep the original (white copy) and second (pink copy). The original (white copy) will be returned to USPS for signature capture. The MPO or servicing Post Office will retain the second copy (pink copy). The Mail Clerk will receive the third copy (yellow copy) with the mail piece. The Mail Clerk will ensure the accountable mail piece(s) are all listed on PS Form 3883 and are in good condition. If the wrapper or container is damaged/torn, the Mail Clerk will not accept the items until they are repaired and properly endorsed by the servicing post office. Keeping a chain of receipt is paramount in dealing with official accountable mail. The current PS Form 3883, dated February 2002, does not have a space for Mail Clerk signature. However, a signature must be obtained from the Mail Clerk in order to show a continuous chain receipts. It is suggested blocks 19 and 20 of the current PS Form 3883 be utilized for this purpose. Print mail clerks name in block 19 and have the mail clerk sign block 20. PS forms 3883 will be retained in the Unit Mailroom/MDC per reference (b) SSIC 5110.1b.

(4) Upon returning to the Unit Mailroom/MDC, the Mail Clerk will list accountable mail items on PS Form 3883. If a Mail Clerk is relieved by another Mail Clerk, the New Mail Clerk will receipt for the accountable mail by filling out the form in the appropriate blocks and sign for it. The relieving mail clerk will then fill out a PS Form 3883 and deliver the accountable mail piece to an authorized agent.

(5) When a Return Receipt (PS Form 3811) is attached to the accountable mail piece, the Mail Clerk shall sign and date this form as the authorized agent.

(6) Accountable mail shall not be kept overnight in the Unit Mailroom/MDC. It will be returned to the servicing post office. When accountable mail is returned, the Mail Clerk will complete a new PS Form 3883 and a postal clerk will sign for the accountable mail. At the discretion of the base postal officer, authorization to hold accountable mail overnight in the Unit Mailroom/MDC may be granted to those mail rooms significantly distant from the servicing post office.

(7) The Unit Postal Officer will verify the delivery of all accountable mail daily to ensure delivery has been made to an authorized agent by initialing the PS Form 3883 on the day of delivery.

(8) Commands are required by paragraph 10-1(3) of OPNAVINST 5510.1G, reference (d), to establish a classified material screening point and must include procedures for screening all registered and certified mail for classified material in the unit's mail handling instructions.

4. Mail Service to Confined Personnel

a. Correctional Facility. Mail privileges extended to prisoners confined for disciplinary reasons shall conform to the current edition of SECNAVINST 1640.9C, reference (e). Outgoing mail from confined personnel shall not bear any obvious external indications that the individual is confined in a correctional facility, including the return address. Mail clerks will indicate a box number, building number, or other identification that does not indicate a confinement facility when forwarding mail to prisoners.

b. In Hands of Civilian Authorities (IHCA). Place all mail for personnel confined by civilian authorities into an official mail envelope addressed to the person in charge of the facility and include a letter of explanation from the command. If you cannot verify that the individual is still confined at the facility, include a Business Reply Mail envelope addressed back to the command.

5. Handling Mail for Casualties

a. Under no circumstances will mail for casualties be returned to sender or forwarded to next of kin (NOK) until absolute verification is received that the next of kin have been notified. Once the NOK have been notified, the servicing Post Office will forward mail to the NOK, or return to sender per the wishes of the NOK. Verification can be obtained from the parent command or the following:

U.S. Marine Corps, Casualty Section, Commercial (703)-784-9512 DSN 278-9512 or 1-800-847-1597

U.S. Navy, Casualty Section, Commercial (901) 874-3202 DSN 368-3202 or 1-800 882-4297

U.S. Air Force, Casualty Section, Commercial (210) 565-3505 DSN 665-3505 or 1-800-433-0048

U.S. Army, Casualty Section, Commercial (703) 325-7990 DSN 221-7990 or 1-800-626-3317

This mail may be held as long as necessary to preclude inadvertent disclosure of casualty status prior to official notification of the NOK. Once the NOK have been notified, mail will be returned to sender or forwarded to NOK per their wishes. In no case will the Unit Mailroom/MDC personnel write any message on the envelope to indicate that the individual is a casualty.

    b. Mail for casualties will be endorsed by the servicing postal activity.

6. Outgoing Mail. Outgoing personal mail shall be deposited in local USPS mail collection boxes or presented to local post offices for mailing. Unit mail clerks/orderlies will not collect outgoing personal mail or have access to USPS collection box keys. Units that are isolated from the MPO and not serviced by USPS may request a waiver in writing (with justification) to this policy from the serving Installation Postal Officer or local USPS Postmaster to collect outgoing personal mail.

| United States Postal Service® | | Today's Date | Sender's Name |

Sorry We Missed You! We Re Deliver for You

| Item is at: | Available for Pick-Up After | **We will redeliver or you or your agent can pick up. See reverse.** |

____ Post Office (See back)

____ _____ Date: ____ Time: ____

☐ **If checked, you or your agent must be present at time of delivery to sign for item.**

Article Number(s)

____ Letter	**For Delivery:** *(Enter total number of items delivered by service type)*
____ Large envelope, magazine, catalog, etc.	**For Notice Left:** *(Check applicable item)*
	____ Express Mail®	____ Insured Mail
____ Parcel	____ Certified Mail™	____ Return Receipt for Merchandise
____ Restricted Delivery	____ Firm Bill	____ Delivery Confirmation
____ Perishable Item	____ Registered Mail™	____ Signature Confirmation
____ Other:		

Notice Left Section

| Article Requiring Payment | Amount Due | Customer Name and Address |

☐ Postage Due ☐ COD ☐ Customs $ ____

☐ **Final Notice:** Article will be returned to sender on

Delivered By and Date

PS Form **3849**, May 2008   *usps.com*   Delivery Notice/Reminder/Receipt

(FRONT)

We will redeliver OR you or your agent can pick up your mail at the Post Office. *(Bring this form and proper ID. If your agent will pick up, sign blow in item 2, and enter agent name here):*

1. a. Check all that apply in section 3; b. Sign in section 2 below; c. leave this notice where the carrier can see it.

2. **Sign Here to authorize redelivery or to authorize an agent to sign for you:**

3. ☐ **Redeliver** *(Enter day of week.):*

(Allow at least two delivery days for redelivery, or go to usps.com/redelivery or call your Post Office to arrange redelivery.)

☐ **Leave item at my address**

(Specify where to leave. Example: "porch," "side door." This option is not available if box is checked on the front requiring you signature at time of delivery.

☐ **Refused** ☐ Forward ☐ Return

Delivery Section

Signature **X**

Printed Name

Delivery Address

USPS |||| ||||| || ||||||||

PS Form **3849**, May 2008 *(Reverse)*   5293 0260 9515 4339

(BACK)

Figure 4-1.--PS Form 3849 (Deliver/Notice/Receipt)

```
                        (Organization Heading)

                                                   SSIC
                                                   Originator code
                                                   Date

From:   Commanding Officer
To:     Personnel authorized to receive and open all official mail to
        include official accountable mail.

Subj:   AUTHORIZATION TO RECEIPT FOR AND OPEN ALL OFFICIAL MAIL TO INCLUDE
        OFFICIAL ACCOUNTABLE MAIL

1.  You are authorized to receipt for and open all official mail including
official accountable mail addressed to the Commanding Officer (name of
organization).

            NAME                              SIGNATURES


(1)  _____            _____

(2)  _____            _____

(3)  _____            _____

(4)  _____            _____

(5)  _____            _____

2.  This authority supersedes all previous authorizations.


                              I.M. Commanding
                              I.M. COMMANDING


Signed copy to:
Unit Mailclerk
```

Figure 4-2.--Sample Letter of Authorization

United States Postal Service®
Firm Delivery Receipt for
Accountable and Bulk Delivery Mail

||||||||||||||||||||||||||||||||

5199 9990 0007 3924 2721

☒ Certified	Delivery	☐ Express Mail®	☐ Recorded Delivery	Return	Signature	Mail for/Bill Number
	☐ Confirmation™	Service		☐ Receipt for	☐ Confirmation™	UNIT/001
☐ COD	Service	☐ Insured	☐ Registered	Merchandise	Service	

Article Number	* Code	Office of Origin (International)	Article Number	* Code	Office of Origin (International)
1. 7705123456789123		Quantico, Va	11.		
2.			12.		
3.			13.		
4.			14.		
5.			15.		
6.			16.		
7.			17.		
8.			18.		
9.			19. CLERK PRINT NAME:		
10.			20. CLERK SIGNATURE:		

* CODE: DC = Received In Damaged Condition. R = Return Receipt Requested. RS = Returned to Sender

Date of Delivery	Number of pieces described above	Recipient signs Form 3849	Postmark – Delivery Office
071015 (Clerk/Carrier) Sgt Postal	1	ERM sites: send Form 3849 to CFS MRM sites: send Form 3849 with form 3883	*Military Post Office* 24 Oct 2007 MCBH 96863
Form 3849 Barcode Number			

PS Form **3883**, February 2002   ─ Delivery

♦ **Follow proper scanning procedures for all articles.**

Figure 4-3.--PS Form 3883 (Firm Delivery Receipt for Accountable and Bulk
Delivery Mail)

Chapter 5

Mail Delivery Receptacles

1. <u>General</u>. The delivery of mail through mail receptacles commonly referred to as Mail Boxes or Post Office Boxes is another method Commanding Officers can provide the delivery of mail to their personnel. The procurement, installation, maintenance, and operation of these mail boxes are the responsibility of the Commanding Officer. Commanding Officer who desire to use receptacles in their Unit Mailroom/MDC will have to coordinate with the Installation Postal Officer to establish addresses that conform to USPS addressing standards. The Installation Postal Officer will provide training and monthly/quarterly inspections of the Unit Mailroom/MDC(s).

2. <u>Assignment of Receptacles</u>

   a. Only assign receptacles to members of the command authorized to receive mail through the Military Postal System (MPS) or United States Postal System (USPS).

   b. Only assign receptacles to members of the command who reside in the barracks or to personnel where USPS does not provide mail delivery service. Exceptions may be granted to personnel whose duties prohibit receipt of mail at their quarters. These exceptions include, but are not limited to, medical doctors, dentists, lawyers, chaplains, or personnel who are legally separated, pending divorce, or other situations where the Commanding Officer feels it is in the best interest of the command. Receptacles cannot be used to conduct private business under any circumstances.

   c. Do not assign the receptacle to more than one person.

   d. Rows of receptacles may be closed out if this simplifies casing the mail and the receptacles are not needed. Under normal operations, rows of receptacles are closed out by attrition, rather than reassigning new boxes.

   e. Assign receptacles that have not been used the longest first, unless a section or row of receptacles is being closed.

   f. Record the member's name, date of receptacle issue, receptacle combination, and the combination change date on a DD Form 2262, "Receptacle Record" (Figure 5-1). The DD Form 2262 will be retained in accordance with reference (b) SSIC 5110.1b.

   g. Label the rear of each assigned receptacle with the member's name.

   h. Provide the combination or key to the member on DD Form 2263, "Mailing Address/Combination Notice" (Figure 5-2). Advise the sponsor to memorize the combination and to read the general instructions on the form. The combination will not be given to anyone other than the member.

3. Maintenance of Receptacles and Receptacle Records

   a. When installing receptacles, coordinate the number of the boxes with the servicing postal activity to insure the numbers and addresses are not duplicated and are within USPS addressing standards.

   b. Do not make major repairs to receptacles. Facility Engineers are responsible for repairs.

   c. When combination or key lock wheels become difficult to turn, lubricate them by placing a small amount of powdered or flaked graphite on the moving parts of the lock.

   d. Spot-check the receptacle windows and doors frequently for damage.

   e. If a receptacle cannot be secured or if it cannot be repaired within a reasonable amount of time, close it and issue another receptacle to the service member.

   f. Maintain a separate DD Form 2262 for each receptacle.

   g. File forms for assigned receptacles numerically in an active file.

   h. File forms for unassigned receptacles chronologically by closure date in an inactive file.

   i. File forms for unassigned receptacles being closed out numerically in a file marked "Do Not Issue."

4. Checking Assigned Receptacles

   a. Check each assigned receptacle at least monthly for excessive mail accumulation, old mail, or non-use. If mail is accumulating in a receptacle and a DD Form 2258 "Temporary Mail Disposition Instructions" (Figure 5-3) has not been filled out, contact the member or the member's command to determine the individual's status. The DD Form 2258 will be retained in accordance with reference (b) SSIC 5110.1b.

   b. If the member is temporarily or permanently absent, prepare a DD Form 2258 indicating status. If the status is received from a source other than the member (First Sergeant, Section OIC, etc.) enter the name and phone number of the source in the special instructions block. Hold the mail until the member provides instructions. Annotate the mail directory file card and process the mail based on the information received (forward, return to sender, etc.).

   c. If no information can be obtained to provide disposition instructions and the mail is unclaimed for 30 days, return the mail to sender endorsed "UNCLAIMED," close the receptacle, and annotate the directory file card. All mail received after that point will be endorsed "MOVED-LEFT NO FORWARDING ADDRESS," and return the mail to the servicing postal activity. Do not reissue a receptacle to a former member unless proof of MPO privilege status is established. Once reestablished, if the sponsor continually fails to claim mail from the receptacle, close the receptacle and provide the mail through general service.

When providing general delivery service, advise the individual that the mail must be returned to the sender as "UNCLAIMED" if it is not picked up within 15 days of receipt at the servicing postal activity.

5. Keys and Combinations

a. Change the key lock cylinder or combination any time a key or combination is believed to be compromised and when a receptacle is withdrawn.

b. Record the member's name, date of receptacle issue, and the serial number of the key or the combination on the DD Form 2262. The DD Form 2262 will be retained in accordance with reference (b) SSIC 5110.1b.

c. Supervisors must ensure an adequate supply of key lock cylinders are retained where key-type receptacles are installed. Cylinders may be rotated with other separate nests of receptacles; however, do not use a cylinder removed from a nest of receptacles in the same nest again for at least three months.

d. Activities issuing the receptacle must replace worn, lost, or broken keys to the receptacle without charge to the customer. Retain at least two duplicate keys for each receptacle. The combination entered on the DD Form 2262 is the only combination retained. Keep duplicate keys and combinations in a safe place out of the patron's reach.

6. Delivery of Mail Through Receptacles

a. Only place matter bearing postage or matter authorized by the Military Postal Service Agency (MPSA) or HQMC (CODE MRP-3) in mail delivery receptacles.

b. Compare the name on the mail or matter with the name label on the receptacle before placing the mail in the receptacle. When names do not match, check the mail piece against the directory and process accordingly. Do not deliver mail addressed to "Occupant" or "Resident" of a receptacle number. Endorse it with "INSUFFICIENT ADDRESS" and return the mail to the servicing postal activity. Mail addressed to the "Commanding Officer of" an individual must be delivered as official mail to the Commanding Officer. Mail addressed to "Commander of a receptacle number", that does not contain an addressee name or unit designation, must be endorsed with "INSUFFICIENT ADDRESS" and returned to sender.

c. When delivering articles that are too large to fit in a receptacle, store them for easy retrieval. Use PS Form 3907 "Post Office Box Mail Pick Up Notice" (Figure 5-4) to notify customers of this mail. Prepare the form the same day the article is received by entering the receptacle number, date, and last name of the addressee on the form. These forms may be laminated to conserve on the number used. Draw a line through previous entries before reusing the forms. These forms may be altered to reflect the hours of operation of the mail distribution point to enhance customer service. Alternate forms and methods of notification may be used to notify customers to enhance the timely delivery of mail. PS Forms 3907 are retained per reference (b) SSIC 5110.12.

d. Use DD Form 2258 for marking receptacles of members who are absent temporarily for any reason. Members must sign this form, when possible, to show the forwarding address or provide disposition instructions for their mail. If a change in status is received from a source other than the member, note the source on the form and the disposition instructions on the form. The member may designate in writing someone to receive their mail during periods of absence as long as that person is an authorized MPO user. If mail accumulates and will not fit in the receptacle, bundle the mail and follow the procedures outlined in paragraph 3 above.

e. Customers may use DD Forms 2258 for a period of no longer than 90 days from the effective date. If a customer will be absent longer than 90 days, a forwarding address must be provided and the receptacle will be closed. When the customer returns after 90 days or more, a new receptacle will be issued.

f. There is no limit to the number of times a customer may use a DD Form 2258; however, using consecutive DD Forms 2258 for the purpose of holding mail in a receptacle for longer than 90 consecutive days is not authorized.

g. Handle mail for members who are in confinement, UA, or casualties per Chapter 6 of this Order. Use DD Form 2258 to mark the receptacle, indicating the member's status until the receptacle is closed or the member's status changes.

7. <u>Withdrawal of Receptacles</u>

a. Remove all mail from the receptacle and route it to the directory section.

b. Remove the name label and block the rear of the receptacle with PS Item0-53A, "Closures, Lockbox, Number 1" or other suitable device.

c. Remove the DD Form 2262 from the active file and record the date of the receptacle closure.

d. Change the key lock cylinder or combination and record the key serial number or new combination and the date of the change on the DD Form 2262. Key lock cylinders or combinations must be changed within 5 days after closing the receptacle.

RECEPTACLE RECORD		1. PS FORM 3801 DATA		2. RECEPTACLE NUMBER
		☐ ON FILE	☐ NOT ON FILE	
3. NAME OF RECEPTACLE HOLDER *(Last, First, Middle Initial)*	4. DATE ISSUED *(YYYYMMDD)*	5. RECEPTACLE COMBINATION	6. DATE CLOSED *(YYYYMMDD)*	7. DATE COMBINATION CHANGED *(YYYYMMDD)*
KING, JOE P.	040915	01-23-45	070914	070915
MARINE, MARCUS J.	071005	67-89-10		

DD FORM 2262, JUN 2000   PREVIOUS EDITION IS OBSOLETE

(FRONT)

INSTRUCTIONS

1. All entries must be typed or printed.

2. PS Form 3801 Data. Indicate by inserting an "X" in the appropriate box.

3. Issue of Receptacle. Type or print name of receptacle holder and date issued.

4. Closure of Receptacle. Enter the date of closure and the date combination was changed (combination must be changed within five duty days from date of closure). Enter the new combination below the old combination.

5. File the receptacle record at the rear of the file (inactive) and issue the receptacles that have been closed the longest.

6. Maintain a current record of receptacle maintenance data, i.e., repairs, etc., and maintain a separate section in the file for damaged receptacles awaiting maintenance.

RECEPTACLE MAINTENANCE RECORD

8. DATE *(YYYYMMDD)*	9. TYPE OF MAINTENANCE

DD FORM 2262 (BACK), JUN 2000

(BACK)

Figure 5-1.--DD Form 2262 (Receptacle Card)

```
┌─────────────────────────────────────────────┐
│  MAILING ADDRESS/COMBINATION NOTICE          │
│                                              │
│  1. Your Complete Mailing Address Is:        │
│                                              │
│     PSC 557 BOX 001                          │
│     FPO AP 96379-0001                        │
│                                              │
│  2. General Instructions:                    │
│                                              │
│     a. Check your receptacle daily.          │
│                                              │
│     b. Notify all correspondents and         │
│        publishers of your correct mailing    │
│        address.                              │
│                                              │
│     c. Do not allow unauthorized personnel   │
│        overseas to receive mail through your │
│        receptacle.                           │
│                                              │
│     d. Do not place or store items in the    │
│        receptacle; it is issued only so you  │
│        can receive mail placed there.        │
│                                              │
│     e. Promptly advise your local facility   │
│        of any temporary or permanent change  │
│        in status, i.e., leave, TDY, TAD,     │
│        reassignment, etc.                    │
│                                              │
│     f. Any component member of your family   │
│        who has a valid ID card may be given  │
│        the receptacle combination or any     │
│        mail addressed to the family except   │
│        restricted delivery mail. However,    │
│        you may state in writing that no      │
│        member other than yourself is         │
│        authorized access to the receptacle   │
│        combination or mail placed therein.   │
└─────────────────────────────────────────────┘
```

(To avoid compromise of your combination, memorize and destroy this portion).

3. Your Combination is: 67-89-10

4. How to Open:

   a. Turn dial indicator left/right three times and stop at: 67

   b. Turn dial left/right pass first combination number and stop at: 89

   c. Turn dial left/right stopping at: 10

   d. Turn latch key left/right to open.

DD FORM 2263, JAN 82   REPLACES AF FORM 1852 WHICH WILL BE USED.

Figure 5-2.--DD Form 2263 (Mailing Address/Combination Notice)

TEMPORARY MAIL DISPOSITION INSTRUCTIONS

-------------------------------- FOLD --------------------------------

NAME (Last, First, MI) (Print):	RECEPTACLE NUMBER
MARINE, MARCUS J.	001

STATUS

ADV ASG	X	LEAVE		CONFINED	
TDY		HOSPITAL		AWOL	

EFFECTIVE DATES TO FWD OR HOLD MAIL (Yr, Mo, Day)

FROM: 071218   TO: 080106

	FORWARD ALL MAIL	X	HOLD ALL MAIL

FORWARD ONLY

	LETTERS		PARCELS		NEWSPAPER/MAG
	PAYCHECK(S)		OTHER *(Use Spec Inst)*		

COMPLETE FORWARDING ADDRESS:

SPECIAL INSTRUCTIONS:

ON LEAVE STATESIDE, HOLD ALL MY MAIL
UNTIL MY RETURN.

SIGNATURE OF RECEPTACLE HOLDER	DATE (Yr, Mo, Day)
Marcus J. Marine	071217

-------------------------------- FOLD --------------------------------

**FOR ADVANCE RECEPTACLE ASGN,
LIST NAME OF SPONSOR AND
DUTY PHONE IN THE SPECIAL
INSTRUCTIONS BLOCK**

DD FORM 2258, JAN 82

Figure 5-3.--DD Form 2258 (Temporary Mail Disposition Instructions)

Post Office Box - - Mail Pickup Notice
Notificacion para reclamar correspondencia

Please give this notice to a clerk during regular business hours. We are holding some of your mail for the reason(s) indicated below:

Por favor entregue esta notificacion al empleado de la ventanilla durante las horas laborables. Tenemos correspondencia para reclamar en la ventanilla de servicio debido a que:

☐ The article is too large for your box
   El articulo es demasiado grande para su apartado

☐ There is too much mail to fit into your box
   Hay demasiado correspondencia para acomodar en su apartado

☐ Poastage due
   Se debe franqueo

☐ The mail requires a signature
   La correspondencia requiere una firma

PS Form **3907**, December 1993

Figure 5-4.--PS Form 3907 (Post Office Box Mail Pick Up Notice)

Chapter 6

Directory

1. <u>General</u>. Accurate and timely directory service is an important mail handling responsibility. Transferred personnel should receive their mail as soon as possible. The individual service member is responsible for providing current directory file information to the Unit Mailroom/MDC when checking in and out. The command will ensure all personnel checks in and out with the Unit Mailroom/MDC.

2. <u>Transferred Personnel</u>. All service members being transferred are required to check out with the Unit Mailroom/MDC and provide a forwarding address or instructions on how to handle any mail received after transfer. Failure to do so may result in the delay of forwarding or delivery of their mail. The Unit Mail Clerk shall provide the individual checking into the unit with a OPNAV 5110/5 (Change of Address Card) (Figure 6-1). The Mail Clerk will send the change of address card to the individual's previous command to update their directory file records.

3. <u>Directory File System</u>. Marine Corps commands will maintain a directory file system for all personnel attached to the unit.

    a. Mail Clerks will fill out a NAVMC 10572 (Directory File Card) with information the service member provides when checking in or checking out. The unit diary is the preferred source document that should be used to extract information to complete the directory file for service members who fail to check in/out of the Unit Mailroom/MDC. Directory File Cards shall be utilized as follows:

        (1) When a service member checks in, enter the following information on the directory file card; last name, first name, middle initial, social security number, grade, unit joined from (complete address not required), date, and unit/section to which assigned (or other information necessary to ensure mail delivery). (See Figure 6-2)

        (2) Temporary changes in status are recorded in the appropriate spaces on the directory file card. Temporary changes such as temporary additional duty (TAD), sick (SK), unauthorized absence (UA), confinement (CONF), or in hands of civilian authorities (IHCA) are entered when applicable. Leave entries are not required on the directory file card.

        (3) When a service member checks out, enter the following information on the directory file card; new complete military address, including an estimated date of arrival (EDA), or a complete home address and have the service member sign and date the card. When a service member cannot or does not provide a forwarding address, this information can be located on the unit diary. A unit diary number must be entered on the card only when the unit diary is used as the source of information to forward mail (See Figure 6-3). The unit diary will be utilized to forward mail to military addresses only.

        (4) When a change of address card is received from a previously transferred service member, the Mail Clerk will check to see if there is a change to the forwarding address previously recorded on the directory file

card. If there is a change in address the Mail Clerk will write the new address into the "new duty station" block of the directory file card if space permits. If space does not permit writing the new address, write "See CAC." The section of the change of address card containing the old unit address, the new address, the signature, and date will be cut out and stapled or taped to the back of the directory file card to show the new forwarding address. This procedure guarantees the source document for the change of address by showing the service member's signature is retained with the new address (See Figure 6-4).

(5) All Unit Mailroom/MDC will provide directory service for all "No Record" First Class Mail to include Priority Mail by utilizing the Marine Corps Total Force System 3270 (MCTFS) or Postal Automated Locator System (PALS). Post office mail room inspectors and directory sections will ensure compliance. In addition, servicing post offices will check all mail identified above to ensure directory service is performed. If service members cannot be located using MCTFS or PALS, Unit Mailroom/MDC(s) will endorse "No Record" First Class Mail in the following manner: NO RECORD 3270 OR PALS, DATE, MAIL CLERK CARD NUMBER, AND UNIT. Other guidelines include: NR = No Record, MLNFA = Moved Left No Forwarding Address, MS = Missent, and FWD = Forward.

(6) Deserters. When a service member is declared a deserter, return to sender all mail with the endorsement "Moved Left No Forwarding Address" (MLNFA). The mail clerk will enter the following information on the directory file card: write the word "Deserter" in the new duty station block, enter the desertion date, and discard date. The unit diary will be used as the source document for this entry. Enter the unit diary number in the appropriate block (See Figure 6-5).

b. Retention Periods

(1) Unit Mailroom/MDC(s) shall retain the directory file cards in accordance with reference (b) SSIC 5110.1b after detachment of all permanently assigned service members. All directory file cards will be maintained in accordance with reference (d). (See Figure 6-3).

(2) Directory file cards for service members in a temporary status attached to a unit for six months or less will be maintained per reference (b) SSIC 5110.1b.

(3) The Mail Clerk will purge the directory file cards during the first week of each month and destroy all cards containing a discard date for that month.

4. Readdressing Mail. Mail Clerks will endorse all mail requiring directory service as shown in Figure 6-6. A diagonal line must be drawn through the incorrect portion of the address and place the correct address to the right of the original address, including an EDA if the new address is a military unit. Permanent mailing addresses going to a civilian location are not authorized to be obtained from the unit diary. If the Marine has not provided proper forwarding instructions and a new military address is not available, mail will be returned to the MPO with the endorsement, "Moved Left No Forwarding Address."

5. <u>Sources of Information for Updating the Directory File</u>. The individual service member is responsible for keeping the Unit Mailroom/MDC informed as to their current status to ensure the timely delivery of their mail. The mail room will still require other source documents to provide information when the individual service member does not or cannot provide this information. The unit diary is the best source document to provide this information due to the complete data it maintains on individual service members. When feasible, the Unit Mailroom/MDC will be provided a copy of each unit diary in order to update the directory file cards. The date will be written on the unit diary when it is received in the Unit Mailroom/MDC, when it has been reviewed, and when it is used to update the directory file cards. When the unit diary cannot be provided to the Unit Mailroom/MDC, the command will provide other documentation, such as morning reports, that provide all the necessary information to update the directory file cards.

NOTICE OF CHANGE OF ADDRESS	DATE
OPNAV 5110/5 (Rev 3-90) S/N 0107-LF-0092500	20 SEP 07

NAME (Last, First, Middle)	RANK/RATE	SOCIAL SECURITY NUMBER
Smith, John R.	Cpl	Not Required

PRIVACY ACT STATEMENT: Authority: Title 39 USC and DoD/US Postal Service Agreement, 2 Feb 59

PRINCIPLE PURPOSES: To route or forward (directory) mail. ROUTINE USES: Use by military and civilian personnel in mail functions.

Data are inspected by commanders, postal officers, and military and civilian inspectors. Disclosure is voluntary; however, failure to

Provide the requested information could result in inability to forward mail.

NEW ADDRESS (Consult SNDL for address)	OLD ADDRESS (Attach mailing label for publisher)
H&S Bn Alpha Co. (S-3) BOX 555607 1st MLG Camp Pendleton, Ca. 92055-5607	H&S Bn MCB (S-3) UNIT 35002 FPO AP 96379-5002

ESTIMATED REPORTING DATE 21 November 2008 SIGNATURE **John R. Smith**	DEPENDENT'S NAME (If applicable) Connie J. Mary L. Tom E.

FORWARD SECOND CLASS MATTER FOR 60 DAYS			THIS SPACE FOR POSTAL CLERK
ITEM	YES	NO	
MAGAZINES	X		
NEWSPAPERS		X	

*U.S. GPO: 1993-0-0704-079/80671

Figure 6-1.--OPNAV 5110/5 (Change of Address Card)

FOR OFFICIAL USE ONLY – PRIVACY SENSITIVE (when completed)

| NAME (Last, First, Middle Initial)

Smith, John R. | GRADE

CPL | DISCARD DATE (Mo., Yr.) |
|---|---|---|

PRIVACY ACT STATEMENT (PAS): In accordance with the Privacy Act of 1974 (Public Law 93-579 / 5 U.S.C. § 552a), this PAS serves to inform you of the authority and purpose for collection of personal information on this Directory File Card (DFC). Please read before completing the DFC.

AUTHORITY: 5 USC § 301, 10 USC § 5031; 39 USC; and DoD/US Postal Service Agreement, 2 Feb 59.

PRINCIPLE PURPOSE: To route or forward (directory) mail. Collected data will be maintained in a Privacy Act System of Records collection governed by Privacy Act System of Records Notice (PA SORN) NM05000-2: PROGRAM MANAGEMENT AND LOCATOR SYSTEM posted at *http://www.defenselink.mil/privacy/notices/usn/NM05100-5.html* .

ROUTINE USES: Use by military and civilian personnel in mail functions. Data are inspected by commanders, postal officers, and military and civilian inspectors. Non-consent disclosures are made outside the DoD only as allowed by 5 U.S.C. § 552a(b)(1) through (b)(12) and the DoD routine uses published at *http://www.defenselink.mil/privacy/dod_blanket_uses.html* .

DISCLOSURE: Although voluntary, failure to provide the requested information could result in mail not being forwarded to new address.

| JOINED FROM

MCB Camp Butler | DATE
22 Oct 07 | UNIT ASSIGNED

S-3 |
|---|---|---|
| | UD NO.
98-07 | |

DROPPED (New duty station, home address, etc. – complete address with EDA)		
SIGNATURE (Required)	DATE	UD NO. (Only if no signature)

MAIL DIRECTORY FILE CARD (5119) NAVMC 10572 (REV. 08-08) (EF)
SN: 0109-LF-067-0700   U/I: 250 Per PKG   (Previous editions are obsolete)

(FRONT)   **FOUO**

FOR OFFICIAL USE ONLY – PRIVACY SENSITIVE (when completed)

TEMPORARY STATUS (TAD, SK, UA, CONF, IHCA)	TO DATE UD NO.	FROM DATE UD NO.	TEMPORARY STATUS (TAD, SK, UA, CONF, IHCA)	TO DATE UD NO.	FROM DATE UD NO.

(BACK)   **FOUO**

Figure 6-2.--NAVMC 10572 (Mail Directory File Card for a Marine
Checking In)

FOR OFFICIAL USE ONLY – PRIVACY SENSITIVE (when completed)

NAME (Last, First, Middle Initial) Smith, John R.	GRADE CPL	DISCARD DATE (Mo., Yr.) Nov 09

PRIVACY ACT STATEMENT (PAS): In accordance with the Privacy Act of 1974 (Public Law 93-579 / 5 U.S.C. § 552a), this PAS serves to inform you of the authority and purpose for collection of personal information on this Directory File Card (DFC). Please read before completing the DFC.

AUTHORITY: 5 USC § 301, 10 USC § 5031; 39 USC; and DoD/US Postal Service Agreement, 2 Feb 59.

PRINCIPLE PURPOSE: To route or forward (directory) mail. Collected data will be maintained in a Privacy Act System of Records collection governed by Privacy Act System of Records Notice (PA SORN) NM05000-2: PROGRAM MANAGEMENT AND LOCATOR SYSTEM posted at *http://www.defenselink.mil/privacy/notices/usn/NM05100-5.html* .

ROUTINE USES: Use by military and civilian personnel in mail functions. Data are inspected by commanders, postal officers, and military and civilian inspectors. Non-consent disclosures are made outside the DoD only as allowed by 5 U.S.C. § 552a(b)(1) through (b)(12) and the DoD routine uses published at *http://www.defenselink.mil/privacy/dod_blanket_uses.html* .

DISCLOSURE: Although voluntary, failure to provide the requested information could result in mail not being forwarded to new address.

JOINED FROM MCB Camp Butler	DATE 22 Oct 07	UNIT ASSIGNED S-3
	UD NO. 98-07	

DROPPED (New duty station, home address, etc. – complete address with EDA) H&S Co H&S Bn (Supply) EDA: 21 Nov 08 1st MLG Camp Pendleton, CA 92055		
SIGNATURE (Required) **John R. Smith**	DATE 21 Oct 09	UD NO. (Only if no signature)

MAIL DIRECTORY FILE CARD (5119) NAVMC 10572 (REV. 08-08) (EF)
SN: 0109-LF-067-0700 U/I: 250 Per PKG (Previous editions are obsolete)

(FRONT) **FOUO**

FOR OFFICIAL USE ONLY – PRIVACY SENSITIVE (when completed)

TEMPORARY STATUS (TAD, SK, UA, CONF, IHCA)	TO DATE UD NO.	FROM DATE UD NO.	TEMPORARY STATUS (TAD, SK, UA, CONF, IHCA)	TO DATE UD NO.	FROM DATE UD NO.
(SK) Room 26 Naval Hospital Camp Lester	8 Feb 08 39-08	2 Feb 08 33-08			

(BACK) **FOUO**

Figure 6-3.--NAVMC 10572 (Mail Directory File Card for a Marine Checking Out)

FOR OFFICIAL USE ONLY – PRIVACY SENSITIVE (when completed)

NAME (Last, First, Middle Initial)	GRADE	DISCARD DATE (Mo., Yr.)
Smith, John R.	CPL	Nov 09

PRIVACY ACT STATEMENT (PAS): In accordance with the Privacy Act of 1974 (Public Law 93-579 / 5 U.S.C. § 552a), this PAS serves to inform you of the authority and purpose for collection of personal information on this Directory File Card (DFC). Please read before completing the DFC.

AUTHORITY: 5 USC § 301, 10 USC § 5031; 39 USC; and DoD/US Postal Service Agreement, 2 Feb 59.

PRINCIPLE PURPOSE: To route or forward (directory) mail. Collected data will be maintained in a Privacy Act System of Records collection governed by Privacy Act System of Records Notice (PA SORN) NM05000-2: PROGRAM MANAGEMENT AND LOCATOR SYSTEM posted at http://www.defenselink.mil/privacy/notices/usn/NM05100-5.html .

ROUTINE USES: Use by military and civilian personnel in mail functions. Data are inspected by commanders, postal officers, and military and civilian inspectors. Non-consent disclosures are made outside the DoD only as allowed by 5 U.S.C. § 552a(b)(1) through (b)(12) and the DoD routine uses published at http://www.defenselink.mil/privacy/dod_blanket_uses.html .

DISCLOSURE: Although voluntary, failure to provide the requested information could result in mail not being forwarded to new address.

JOINED FROM	DATE	UNIT ASSIGNED
MCB Camp Butler	22 Oct 07	S-3
	UD NO. 98-07	

DROPPED (New duty station, home address, etc. – complete address with EDA)

H&S Co H&S Bn (Supply)   EDA: 21 Nov 08
1st MLG Camp Pendleton, CA 92055   "SEE CAC"

SIGNATURE (Required)	DATE	UD NO. (Only if no signature)
John R. Smith	21 Oct 09	

MAIL DIRECTORY FILE CARD (5119) NAVMC 10572 (REV. 08-08) (EF)
SN: 0109-LF-067-0700   U/I: 250 Per PKG   (Previous editions are obsolete)

(FRONT)   **FOUO**

FOR OFFICIAL USE ONLY – PRIVACY SENSITIVE (when completed)

TEMPORARY STATUS (TAD, SK, UA, CONF, IHCA)	TO DATE / UD NO.	FROM DATE / UD NO.	TEMPORARY STATUS (TAD, SK, UA, CONF, IHCA)	TO DATE / UD NO.	FROM DATE / UD NO.
(SK) Room 26 Naval Hospital Camp Lester					

NEW ADDRESS (Consult SNDL for address)

H&S Bn Alpha Co. (S-3)
BOX 555607
1st MLG
Camp Pendleton, Ca. 92055-5607

OLD ADDRESS (Attach mailing label for publisher)

H&S Bn MCB (S-3)
UNIT 35002
FPO AP 96379-5002

ESTIMATED REPORTING DATE

21 November 2008

DEPENDENT'S NAME (If applicable)

Connie J.
Mary L.
Tom E.

SIGNATURE   **John R. Smith**

FORWARD SECOND CLASS MATTER FOR 60 DAYS

THIS SPACE FOR POSTAL CLERK

ITEM	YES	NO
MAGAZINES	X	
NEWSPAPERS		X

(BACK)   **FOUO**

Figure 6-4.--NAVMC 10572 (Mail Directory File Card for Information
Received from a Change of Address Card)

FOR OFFICIAL USE ONLY – PRIVACY SENSITIVE (when completed)

NAME (Last, First, Middle Initial)	GRADE	DISCARD DATE (Mo., Yr.)
Smith, Michael J.	LCpl	Mar 09

PRIVACY ACT STATEMENT (PAS): In accordance with the Privacy Act of 1974 (Public Law 93-579 / 5 U.S.C. § 552a), this PAS serves to inform you of the authority and purpose for collection of personal information on this Directory File Card (DFC). Please read before completing the DFC.

AUTHORITY: 5 USC § 301, 10 USC § 5031; 39 USC; and DoD/US Postal Service Agreement, 2 Feb 59.

PRINCIPLE PURPOSE: To route or forward (directory) mail. Collected data will be maintained in a Privacy Act System of Records collection governed by Privacy Act System of Records Notice (PA SORN) NM05000-2: PROGRAM MANAGEMENT AND LOCATOR SYSTEM posted at *http://www.defenselink.mil/privacy/notices/usn/NM05100-5.html* .

ROUTINE USES: Use by military and civilian personnel in mail functions. Data are inspected by commanders, postal officers, and military and civilian inspectors. Non-consent disclosures are made outside the DoD only as allowed by 5 U.S.C. § 552a(b)(1) through (b)(12) and the DoD routine uses published at *http://www.defenselink.mil/privacy/dod_blanket_uses.html* .

DISCLOSURE: Although voluntary, failure to provide the requested information could result in mail not being forwarded to new address.

JOINED FROM	DATE 30 Jun 07	UNIT ASSIGNED
MCB Camp Butler	UD NO. 61-07	Supply

DROPPED (New duty station, home address, etc. – complete address with EDA)
Deserter (4 Feb 08)

SIGNATURE (Required)	DATE 4 Feb 08	UD NO. (Only if no signature) 34-08

MAIL DIRECTORY FILE CARD (5119) NAVMC 10572 (REV. 08-08) (EF)
SN: 0109-LF-067-0700   U/I: 250 Per PKG   (Previous editions are obsolete)

(FRONT)   **FOUO**

FOR OFFICIAL USE ONLY – PRIVACY SENSITIVE (when completed)

TEMPORARY STATUS (TAD, SK, UA, CONF, IHCA)	TO DATE UD NO.	FROM DATE UD NO.	TEMPORARY STATUS (TAD, SK, UA, CONF, IHCA)	TO DATE UD NO.	FROM DATE UD NO.
UA		5 Jan 08 04-08			

(BACK)   **FOUO**

Figure 6-5.--NAVMC 10572 (Mail Directory File Card for a Person Declared a "Deserter")

Ms. J.W. Smith
24 Rock St.
Anytown, TX 99999-0000

~~**LCpl B.R. Smith**~~
H&S Co. H&S BN
Camp Lejeune NC 28542-0125

EDA 30 June 2008
3rd MLG
UNIT 35010
FPO AP 96373-5010

Figure 6-6.--Sample Mail Requiring Directory Service